the
Sacred
Clutter–
Clearing

JOURNAL

THIS JOURNAL BELONGS TO

the Sacred Clutter-Clearing

JOURNAL

DISCOVER AND RELEASE THE EMOTIONAL ROOTS OF YOUR CLUTTER AND CREATE SPACE FOR ABUNDANCE, JOY AND GROWTH

DENISE LINN

HAY HOUSE

Carlsbad, California • New York City
London • Sydney • New Delhi

Published in the United Kingdom by:
Hay House UK Ltd, The Sixth Floor, Watson House,
54 Baker Street, London W1U 7BU
Tel: +44 (0)20 3927 7290; Fax: +44 (0)20 3927 7291; www.hayhouse.co.uk

Published in the United States of America by:
Hay House Inc., PO Box 5100, Carlsbad, CA 92018-5100
Tel: (1) 760 431 7695 or (800) 654 5126
Fax: (1) 760 431 6948 or (800) 650 5115; www.hayhouse.com

Published in Australia by:
Hay House Australia Ltd, 18/36 Ralph St, Alexandria NSW 2015
Tel: (61) 2 9669 4299; Fax: (61) 2 9669 4144; www.hayhouse.com.au

Published in India by:
Hay House Publishers India, Muskaan Complex, Plot No.3, B-2,
Vasant Kunj, New Delhi 110 070
Tel: (91) 11 4176 1620; Fax: (91) 11 4176 1630; www.hayhouse.co.in

A catalogue record for this book is available from the British Library.

Tradepaper ISBN: 978-1-83782-220-1

This product uses papers sourced from responsibly managed forests. For more information, see www.hayhouse.co.uk.

Printed and bound by CPI Group (UK) Ltd, Croydon CR0 4YY

If you struggle with clutter, like I do,
this book is dedicated to you.
May your life be filled with clarity and joy!

Contents

part III:
CLUTTER CLEARING FOR YOUR LIFE

INTRODUCTION
Modern-Day Alchemy

Consciously clearing your clutter—which is what this journal will teach you how to do—can kick off a spiral of results that unfold in powerful, profound, even mysterious ways. I call clutter clearing modern-day alchemy because it is one of the fastest ways to spiritually transform your life.

This journal guides you through a process that teaches much more than just the knowledge of how to get rid of stuff you don't need. We'll move room by room in your house and clear what no longer serves you. But we won't stop there—we'll also address those nonphysical things that are cluttering up your life, such as time clutter, relationship clutter, and even your thoughts.

Using this journal may be the most transformative journey you take. Not only will you learn how to clear your space and let go of those things in your life that you don't need, but you will also make space for miracles to abound in your life. Your home is a mirror of yourself, so when you shift the energy of your home, you shift the energy within yourself too. Your health, relationships, and level of abundance all benefit from thoughtfully deciding what you want to keep and what it's time to release. As you do so, you let go of old patterns that have been holding you back.

Think of clearing your clutter as a sacred adventure—a joyous, conscious, spiritual journey toward understanding who you are and why you're on this planet at this time. Prepare to clean the debris from your life and make space for new energy, ideas, ways of being, and developments to flow to you. Even if you think your life is pretty darn good, be open for it to be even better.

My Journey with Clutter Clearing

When I was a little girl, whenever I got sick, my mother would say, "If I clear out your room, you'll feel better." She would take everything out of the room I didn't need and I *would* feel better. Later, in my teens, I had a very traumatic near-death experience after a stranger attacked me when I was out riding my motorbike. While I was in the hospital, my spirit left my body and entered a beautiful, radiant space where everything and everyone was pure energy. When I came back into my body, I could see things other people couldn't see. I saw that everything—people, blades of grass, and even inanimate objects—was comprised of energy. I could now see that there are strands of energy that connect us to other people, animals, plants, and even objects and things.

I began to understand that the things we have in our homes and our lives can either propel us forward—or drag us backward.

After I healed, I spent time with and learned from many indigenous cultures because I could sense that they had a better understanding of the realms I had visited during that hospital stay. I studied with the Zulu in Africa, the Aborigines in Australia, the Maori in New Zealand, the Kahuna in Hawaii, and the Cherokee here in North America (I have Cherokee ancestors). I first began studying feng shui—the Chinese art of enhancing energy through object placement—in the 1980s in Hong Kong. From there, I started writing books, sharing what I was learning about energy, space clearing, and feng shui.

My intent and my prayer is that in the days, weeks, and months ahead as you embark on this journey, you step into a vibrancy, clarity, and radiance unlike anything you've experienced before. And that you let go of not just possessions, but also the patterns, habits, and relationships that don't serve you anymore so that you can step into your power and grace. This can truly be a time of letting go, allowing Spirit in, and stepping into your potential. I am so excited to be on this journey with you, and I'm delighted that we will be co-creating miracles.

Throughout this journal, I will be sharing affirmations—short, positive statements to repeat to yourself as you undertake this work—that will keep your mind and heart open to possibility. Now, as we begin, here is an affirmation to set the tone for our work together: "I am willing to let go of what's not working. I am ready to make a change. I am open to my life expanding."

part

I

BEGINNING YOUR CLUTTER-CLEARING JOURNEY

What Is Clutter?

Clutter is highly individual—what is clutter to one person may not be clutter to another person. To determine if something is clutter, ask yourself these three questions:

- *Do I love it?*
- *Do I use it?*
- *Does it make me feel empowered?*

If the answer is yes to any or all questions, it's not clutter. Clutter is anything you don't love, you don't use, or that makes you feel disempowered.

How could an object make you feel disempowered? Clutter is not always related to the object itself. It can also be about the meaning that you give that object. And if that meaning is less than empowering, that object is clutter. If that meaning is empowering, it's not. For example, if you look at your old high school trophies and they give you a surge of confidence because they remind you of your strengths, they're not clutter. On the other hand, if you look at them and feel sad, wistful, or regretful that you're no longer doing those activities or using those skills that earned you those trophies in the first place, they're disempowering you. In this case, they are clutter.

Here's an incomplete list of things that typically constitute clutter:

- Any object you don't use or love
- Anything that doesn't represent who you are, or who you're becoming
- Items that don't truly fit in the space that you have and that add to physical and visual overwhelm
- Unfinished projects
- Plants that are languishing
- Items that have needed to be repaired for a long time
- Recipes and cookbooks you never refer to

- Half-full containers of makeup, shampoo, or lotions you no longer use
- Expired coupons
- Bottles of expired pills
- Clothes that don't fit, are worn out, or you don't like
- A deceased one's belongings that don't have meaning for you
- Books, magazines, and newspapers you will never get around to reading
- Food you'll never eat
- Clutter isn't always physical. Your time can be cluttered, your computer can be cluttered, your relationships can be cluttered, and so can your own mind.
- Time clutter includes activities, obligations, or habits that crowd out room for rest, renewal, and growth.
- Relationship clutter can mean you are spending too much of your time with people who drain your energy.
- Computer clutter can lead to a sense of overwhelm every time you sit at your desk—this can include too many files or e-mails or too many items on your desktop.
- Mental clutter can be thoughts, beliefs, and sayings that you subconsciously repeat to yourself every day and that negatively impact your mental health.

QUESTIONS

Throughout this journal, I'll ask you questions that will help you reflect on what you're learning and gain more insight into what is, and what isn't, cluttering up your home, your mind, and your life. Let's start that process now by answering these questions:

Now that I know the definition of *clutter*, what items in my home immediately come to mind as being clutter?

What are some items I use, love, and find empowering that might seem like clutter to someone else but are not clutter to me?

What are some things in my life that might be cluttering up my time?

What relationships do I need to look more closely at, because they may be relationship clutter?

What thoughts or beliefs might be cluttering up my mind?

Why We Keep Clutter

We are a supersized society. Although we have smaller families than we did in generations past, we live in bigger houses and have more possessions than ever before. In fact, we have so much stuff that we can't contain it in our homes—1 in every 11 Americans has at least one storage unit.

Why do we have so much stuff? On a practical level, manufacturing has advanced to the point that we can make more things, more cheaply than ever before. As a result, we buy more things than ever, and when those things break or get lost, we simply replace them.

On a deeper level, we typically accumulate things for psychological reasons. Most often we hold on to objects as a form of protection in a misguided attempt to counteract a feeling of emptiness. But research has shown that we are not happier, or healthier, or more vibrant, or more successful because of our stuff. In fact, research reveals just the opposite. We are weighed down by our stuff. We have to trip over it, clean it, take care of it, and pay to store it.

If you go through the exercise of clearing your clutter without understanding why you accumulated so much clutter in the first place, you will likely simply refill your home with new things you don't really need.

To prevent that from happening, take a look at the list of reasons we keep clutter, and check the box next to the ones that apply to you. These are the things that you can devote energy to healing as you clear your clutter, and as you enjoy the extra energy and time you'll have once you are finished.

☐ **Fear of not having enough in the future**
Keeping something because you're afraid you might need it in the future is an affirmation for lack—it's basically saying that you don't trust that your needs will be met in the future. This can become a self-fulfilling prophecy.

- [ ] **A subconscious tendency because clutter runs in your family**
  You may believe that keeping a lot of stuff around is an inherited tendency. But the past does not need to equal the future. You can change.

- [ ] **Sentimentality or nostalgia for the past**
  Whether it's your grandmother's furniture or your child's booties, it can be a burden to own these things, especially if you don't use them or love them, or they make you feel sad or trapped or anything else negative. Take a photo of the item. Make a beautiful scrapbook if there are multiple items, and then you can release these old things and create space and energy for new shifts to occur in your life.

- [ ] **Protection**
  Having a lot of things can feel like a protective force field around you, but it can also keep other people and new ideas and energy away.

- [ ] **Validation**
  All the blue ribbons, trophies, and awards you won when you were in school can be your way of saying, *Here is the evidence that I was once good at something.* Ask yourself, *Do I actually need these objects to verify that I'm enough?* If the answer is yes, keep them. But if the answer is, *Actually, I don't need them—I know that who I am is enough,* release them.

- [ ] **Comfort**
  Sometimes clutter is just comfortable because you've gotten used to it. It's familiar. Change can be scary because it's unknown. Ask yourself, *Do I want my life to stay the exact same as it is for the foreseeable future?*

- [ ] **Desire**

  Some clutter is an affirmation of who you desire to be—for example, the exercise equipment you bought on late-night television because you want to be the kind of person who exercises, but you never use it. Remember that your possessions do not define you. Use them, or clear them out.

- [ ] **A metaphor for life**

  Some people have a home that looks immaculate, but when you open any drawer, cabinet, or closet, it's filled to the brim with clutter. There's an attractive veneer, but beneath the surface there's a lot of stuff being suppressed. When you're looking at your clutter, look to see if there are any metaphors for your life.

- [ ] **Value**

  This typically shows up as "I paid a lot for this" or "It might be worth something someday." Yes, it might, but it might not. Is it really worth it to clog your life in the present because you paid a lot for something in the past, or it might be valuable in the future? Remember, things are only worth what someone will pay you for them. It's true that many items made today are typically of lower quality than those that were made in earlier eras. If it works, you love it, and you use it, it's not clutter. But if you don't use it and are just holding on to it because you think it should be worth something, it's clutter.

- [ ] **Responsibility**

  Sometimes we feel like there's no one else who will take good care of our things, so we keep them even though they're not enhancing our life. Yes, the item may be perfectly good, but do you use it? Do you love it? If the answer is no, you know what I'm going to say—let it go!

☐ **Guilt**

It's natural to feel guilty about getting rid of something you received as a gift. But think of it this way—are you willing to clog your life for the sake of not hurting someone's feelings? Chances are the person who gave you the gift is someone you care for. So if you gave a gift to someone you cared for, would you want them to keep it even if they didn't want it just so they wouldn't hurt your feelings? I'm going to suggest that no, you wouldn't. When someone gives you something, it is yours to do with as you please. If you're concerned that getting rid of that gift you don't use and don't love will hurt someone's feelings, consider stepping into your strength. You don't need to put others' needs before your own needs any longer.

QUESTIONS

Look back at the boxes you checked and take a moment to write down
your thoughts about these reasons and how you can release them.

Why It's Important to Clear Your Clutter

There comes a point when your physical belongings begin to crowd out your spiritual and emotional needs. Yet, because clutter is such a regular and pervasive part of our lives, you may not have fully recognized how much it has been weighing you down. I hope that seeing this long list of the negative effects of clutter will help motivate you to get going—and keep going—on your clutter-clearing journey!

- Increases your levels of stress hormones
- Invites procrastination and decreases your productivity
- Makes you feel disorganized, or even like a failure
- Contributes to a sense that your life is chaotic
- Makes you feel sluggish and tired
- Collects germs and dust
- Creates falling hazards
- Impedes new energy from coming into your life
- Contributes to isolation (especially if you don't want to have people over because your home is cluttered)
- Costs money—to store, to buy something new because you can't find the thing you already own, and because it can prevent you from being able to keep track of your bills so you incur late fees and penalties
- Wastes time—over the course of our lives, we spend roughly six and a half solid months looking for missing objects, which is equivalent to almost 5,000 hours!
- Keeps you tied to the past, preventing you from being in the present moment and creating a better future
- Makes you feel physically, emotionally, and energetically heavy; it can be tied to depression and excess weight

Taking this journey into clutter clearing will not only free up money and time, but also will allow you to have less stress in your life. It's also good for the planet as it will help you repurpose what you already own and buy fewer things in the future. When you address your clutter, the overall effect is that you create space to move beyond whatever has been blocking you and step into freedom, grace, and a fuller expression of who you truly are.

QUESTIONS

Which of these negative effects of clutter have I been experiencing?

What will be possible in my life when I lessen these negative influences of clutter on my life?

Clutter-Clearing Myths

Part of the reason clutter has become such a big part of our lives is that we don't see it clearly. Instead, we believe a lot of things that aren't true about our stuff and what it means. To truly relieve yourself of your clutter, dispel these common myths from your belief system.

To have a harmonious life, you need to be clutter free. You don't need to be a clean freak, a tidy person, or a minimalist for clearing clutter to work for you. I am a longtime messy person—I start things and don't clean up after. I love stuff. But I have come to understand that when I feel stuck, if I clutter clear, everything changes: my energy, the way I feel, and even my life. And even if you have some clutter, you can still have a fabulous life.

If I let go of stuff, I'll lose my connection to the past. The past dwells within you in the form of your memories, the imprint those experiences made on your energy, and even on your DNA (as the science of epigenetics tells us that our experiences influence which of our genes get fully expressed, and which don't). When you let go of objects from the past, you still retain that connection. If there is some piece of your past that you want to release, try relinquishing those objects that represent that time period while imagining cutting the cords that bind you to that past. If there's a part of your past that you do want to maintain your connection to, take photographs of those items and put them in an album. You don't need to keep the things in order to keep the memories.

I have to find a good home for my stuff. Your items are on a journey of their own, just as everything on this earth is on a journey. You do not need to find your objects a good home. Once you give something away, it is on the next leg of its journey, and it's exactly where it needs to be.

If someone gave me something, I'm not a very nice person if I give it away. You do not need to keep everything that everyone gives you. Be gracious when you receive it. Accept it with an open heart. And know that the gift you're receiving is less about the object and more about the sentiment that goes along with it. Receive and keep the love, but if you don't love or use the object, let it go.

QUESTIONS

Are there any of these clutter myths I have bought into?

Am I ready to release these myths from my belief system?

A Journey of Self-Discovery—
Life Assessment

The path to an extraordinary life lies in exploring who you truly are and then fully sharing every aspect of your gift with the world. The questions in this section—especially the uncomfortable and challenging ones—can help you discover who you are.

Some of the questions in this Life Assessment take courage to answer and a willingness to face yourself in an honest and thoughtful way. Know that your work in answering these questions will bring clarity and focus to the clutter clearing that you do. And that there are no right answers—just truthful ones.

ANCESTORS

If you were to think about your ancestors as a collective, what qualities might you imagine they embodied? Do you possess any of these qualities and characteristics? If so, how does this make you feel?

What are your general feelings about your ancestors? And how do you imagine they are impacting your life?

MOTHER'S LIFE

What feelings and/or emotions arise for you when you think about your mother (or another parental figure or caregiver)? List them along with the reasons that you feel you have these emotions.

_____

_____

_____

_____

_____

_____

Have you noticed any patterns—positive and negative—from your mother's life that have occurred in your life?

_____

_____

_____

_____

_____

_____

_____

_____

FATHER'S LIFE

What feelings and/or emotions arise for you when you think about your father (or another parental figure or caregiver)? List them along with the reasons that you feel you have these emotions.

_____

_____

_____

_____

_____

_____

Have you noticed any patterns—positive and negative—from your father's life that have occurred in your life?

_____

_____

_____

_____

_____

_____

_____

_____

_____

YOUR RELATIONSHIPS

Who have been the significant people in your life?

_____

_____

_____

_____

_____

_____

_____

_____

What have you gained from each of these people?

_____

_____

_____

_____

_____

_____

_____

_____

_____

_____

What are the qualities within the people who you admire the most?

_____

_____

_____

_____

_____

_____

_____

How have these qualities shown up in you?

_____

_____

_____

_____

_____

_____

_____

_____

_____

What are the qualities in others that you find most challenging or disdainful?

_____

_____

_____

_____

_____

_____

How have these qualities shown up in you?

_____

_____

_____

_____

_____

_____

_____

_____

_____

_____

Are there any relationships you need to heal or come to terms with, or people you need to forgive? List them and make a plan on how you are going to do this.

YOUR HEALTH AND BODY IMAGE

What is the truth about your current state of health?

How do you feel about your body? What do you think your body says to the world about who you are?

Regarding your health, what would you like to change or improve?
Are you willing to do it? How and when are you going to do it?

YOUR FINANCES

Are you satisfied with your finances? If not, why not?

_____

_____

_____

_____

_____

_____

_____

Are finances a priority for you? If not, what are your priorities?

_____

_____

_____

_____

_____

_____

_____

_____

_____

What beliefs do you hold about money?

What beliefs do you hold about people who have money?

What beliefs do you hold about people who do not have money?

Do these beliefs help or hinder your relationship with money?

Are there family or ancestral patterns that might be attributed to your beliefs about money?

_____

_____

_____

_____

_____

_____

_____

_____

_____

_____

_____

_____

_____

_____

_____

_____

_____

YOUR CREATIVITY

What gives you the greatest joy? What makes your spirit fly?

_____

_____

_____

_____

_____

_____

_____

_____

Are you fulfilling your potential? Why or why not? When will you? How will you?

_____

_____

_____

_____

_____

_____

_____

_____

_____

Is there something creative you've always wanted to do and have yet to take action on?

YOUR EXPERIENCES

What are some of your best early memories? Did you adopt any beliefs about life as a result of these experiences?

_____

_____

_____

_____

_____

_____

_____

_____

_____

What are some of your worst early memories? Did you adopt any beliefs about life as a result of these experiences?

_____

_____

_____

_____

_____

_____

_____

_____

_____

_____

What was your childhood home like? Was it cluttered or was it clear? Was it inviting? Cold? Something else? How do you feel that this might have affected you?

What have been the recurring themes throughout your life?

What emotions continue to cycle again and again in your life?

YOUR HOME

What kind of homes have you lived in?

What makes a house feel like a home?

Are there any recurring patterns in regard to your homes?

_____

_____

_____

_____

_____

_____

_____

_____

Do you feel at home when you are in your current home?
Why or why not?

_____

_____

_____

_____

_____

_____

_____

_____

What are some of your most valued possessions and why?

YOU

What are at least 10 things that make you remarkable or special? List them.

_____

_____

_____

_____

_____

_____

_____

_____

_____

_____

What are at least 10 personal achievements in your life (even learning to drive can be one of them)? List them.

_____

_____

_____

_____

_____

_____

_____

_____

_____

What are at least 10 things that you can do well (even the thorough way you brush your teeth can be one of them)? List them.

If you had absolutely no limits (physically, emotionally, financially, or in any arena), what would you do with your life?

Do you have any negative habits? Do you accept yourself unconditionally, in spite of these patterns?

Are there things in your life that you know you should be doing (and you want to be doing) but aren't?

Are there things in your life that you know you shouldn't be doing, but you do them anyway?

What or who do you judge? (Do any of these qualities exist within you?)

What makes you sad, angry, frustrated, irritated, depressed, afraid, guilty, resentful, ashamed, and/or upset? Make a list.

_____

_____

_____

_____

_____

_____

_____

_____

What makes you happy, joyous, relaxed, peaceful, content, excited, and/or connected to Spirit? Make a list.

_____

_____

_____

_____

_____

_____

_____

_____

How would you describe yourself in five words?

What are your top values? Are you being true to them? Is your life congruent with your values?

Is there anything that you do to please others, to your own detriment?

_____

_____

_____

_____

_____

_____

_____

_____

Is there anything that you do out of obligation, rather than out of joy?

_____

_____

_____

_____

_____

_____

_____

_____

_____

Is there something that you feel stops you from expanding and/or succeeding even more?

_____

_____

_____

_____

_____

_____

_____

What seems to drive your life? (for example the need to be loved or feel significant, included, important, free, etc.)

_____

_____

_____

_____

_____

_____

_____

_____

YOUR DREAMS

If you never had to work and could do anything that you like with your time, what would you do?

_____

_____

_____

_____

_____

_____

_____

_____

What would a perfect day be for you, starting with when you wake up until the next morning?

_____

_____

_____

_____

_____

_____

_____

_____

_____

_____

What would be the perfect vacation for you?

_____

_____

_____

_____

_____

_____

_____

_____

What would you love to be doing in 5, 10, and 20 years?

_____

_____

_____

_____

_____

_____

_____

_____

What goals do you have in life (for your health, career, relationships, creativity, abundance, and connection to Spirit)?

MAKING CHANGES

If there was one aspect of yourself that you could change right now, what would it be?

What is one small step you could take to make that wish come true?

By answering these questions, you can step into a spiritual understanding of the deeper issues at play in your clutter clearing. They prepare you for the true alchemy of clearing your clutter.

The Energy of Clutter

Every object you have in your home affects your energy field. It either raises your energy, lowers it, or keeps it neutral. That's in part because objects can hold residual energy—any time there has been any intense emotion around an object, it's not uncommon for that object to absorb it.

Clutter also activates various emotions. For example, let's say there's something broken that your spouse said they would fix, but it's been several months. Subconsciously, every time you see that unfixed item, it might trigger a bit of anger. Or maybe your grandmother gave you a beautiful crystal before she passed. Now, every time you see that crystal you feel sad. Or say you borrowed a book from someone that you never returned. Subliminally, every time you see that book, you experience a little pang of guilt.

Clutter can also have associations. You could associate an object with who gave it to you, the store where you bought it, what the day was like on the day you bought it, or if the salesperson was rude or pleasant. None of these associations are bad or good, per se, but they are influencing you even though you may not be aware of them.

The hundreds of items in your home are radiating energy that you absorb and then send out into the world. It is not about the objects, it's about the meaning, even if you don't consciously know what the meaning is. That's why a huge step in the clutter-clearing process is to raise your awareness of the belongings you have in your home and how those items are affecting you.

QUESTIONS

Think of one specific item in your home, and then write down the
various emotions, associations, and meanings that object might
represent.

The Meanings of Your Objects

As humans, we assign meaning to everything, including the objects in our homes. As you consider whether you love the objects you own and if they are empowering or disempowering, take into account the many things those objects can represent:

- The person who gave it to you

- The person who made it

- The place where you bought it

- The people who have owned it

- The circumstances in your life at the time that you acquired it

- The meaning it had for the person who gave it to you

- Your memories associated with the item

- What it makes you think of

- The intangible things that item represents

Guided Visualization:
A Journey to Your Future

Try this exercise to raise your awareness of the current energy in your home and your life, and to plant a seed of where you are headed—the future you are creating by going through the process of clearing your clutter.

Start by taking a deep breath and allowing your eyes to close.

For a few moments, focus your awareness on your breath. With every exhalation, feel yourself relaxing. Your shoulders are dropping. Those small muscles in your forehead are relaxing. With every breath you take, you find a wonderful wave of relaxation rolling through you. It is safe to let go.

Then imagine that you're standing outside your front door. What do you feel in that space? What messages about the people who live behind that front door can you perceive? Simply feel the energy.

Now imagine that you are reaching your hand out and touching the doorknob—the equivalent of shaking hands with your home. What feeling do you get from this interaction?

Now imagine opening the door. As you step across the threshold, you develop the ability to sense energy. You can tell if something raises your energy, lowers your energy, or keeps it neutral.

As you are exploring your home in your mind, notice if there are some areas that feel stuck or cluttered. You can travel through your home assessing the energy quickly and easily. If you have a basement, an attic, or garage, don't forget to explore those areas too.

Now let all of that go and travel forward in time to a positive future. See yourself in the future feeling great. You can be anywhere in this future vision—the park, the beach, your home that has been cleared of its clutter. Sense how good it feels to be who you are, because you know everything in your life is going so well.

Really savor how you feel in this positive vision of the future. Exaggerate the feeling so that it gets imprinted in your cells. This is who you are becoming. This is who you are.

All that you do in the days and weeks and months ahead to clear out and let go of anything you no longer need will propel you toward this vision. This is your destiny. And it's so good.

Finish by taking a few deep breaths. Know that all is well. That your path is guided. That everything you do in the days ahead moves you toward this beautiful, compelling future.

Then bring yourself back to normal, waking awareness. You've done so well. You have planted a seed—a seed that will sprout and bear delicious fruit. Let this envisioning compel you forward, into action.

QUESTIONS

What messages did I receive about the energy of my home?

_____

_____

_____

_____

_____

_____

_____

_____

_____

_____

_____

_____

What parts of my home felt the most cluttered in my visualization?

_____

_____

_____

_____

_____

_____

_____

What parts held the most positive energy?

_____

_____

_____

_____

_____

_____

_____

_____

_____

Where was I in my positive vision of the future?

_____

_____

_____

_____

_____

_____

_____

_____

What sights, smells, and feelings were present?

_____

_____

_____

_____

_____

_____

_____

_____

_____

_____

Start Small: Clear One Thing with Intention

The clarity and good feelings that clearing clutter provides are available to you anytime you are feeling off, down, or unfocused. You don't have to do a major clutter-clearing session—you can always clear just one thing. And when you clear one thing with a specific intention, the benefits of your actions intensify.

Here's an example: Let's say your Aunt Mabel gave you a small painting that you didn't like, but you didn't want to hurt her feelings, so instead of getting rid of it, you decided to stick it in a drawer in case she came over (and you could then pull it out of the drawer and display it during her visit). But your Aunt Mabel passed on three years ago, and the painting is still in your drawer. You don't use it, don't love it, and every time you see it, it brings your energy down because you feel guilty that you never liked this gift. In other words, it's clutter.

To clear this item with intention, think about what getting rid of it will make possible for you. That is your intention. In this example, because the painting carries an energy of not wanting to do something that someone else might disapprove of, you could set an intention for being self-confident and not needing the approval of others. When you find a new home for the painting, do it with the intention of welcoming more self-acceptance into your life.

To start shifting your energy today, and to build your clutter-clearing muscles, choose just one item, and then clear it with intention.

QUESTIONS

What one item is a good candidate for this exercise?

_____

_____

_____

_____

_____

_____

_____

What is the deeper meaning of this object?

_____

_____

_____

_____

_____

_____

_____

_____

_____

_____

Does this item have any messages for me?

_____

_____

_____

_____

_____

_____

_____

_____

What is my intention in clearing this item?

_____

_____

_____

_____

_____

_____

_____

_____

_____

_____

_____

_____

What possibilities am I hoping that clearing this object will open up in my life?

_____

_____

_____

_____

_____

_____

_____

_____

After cleaning this one item with intention, capture the results here:

How do I feel now that I have cleared this object?

_____

_____

_____

_____

_____

_____

_____

_____

What happened afterward?

Collage for Change

The clutter clearing you do in your home is about more than releasing what's not working. It's also a powerful way to propel you forward toward your goals, desires, and dreams.

Before you begin your room-by-room clutter clearing, it's helpful to create a collage of images that remind you of those intangible things you are seeking to create. Think of it as a ceremony that will set the tone and intention for your clutter clearing. Any ceremony gives form to the formless. And this particular ceremony puts your dreams and desires into visual form so that you can focus on what you are seeking and steep in the energy of those results, which helps draw them to you.

To create this collage, you'll need to answer a few questions first:

Why do I want to clear my clutter?

What am I seeking to create?

How do I desire to feel in the future—what specific emotions or states of being do I want to inhabit? (some possibilities include strong, relaxed, content, abundant, joyous, and free)

Once you have your answers to these questions, search through books, magazines, and newspapers, and compile a stack of images, words, and phrases that give you those feelings. Arrange them on a large piece of paper or poster board in a way that feels right to you, and then glue them down.

When your collage is finished, put your hands onto the paper and say a blessing, prayer, or affirmation. This doesn't need to be religious—it can be something as simple as "May my life be filled with goodness" or whatever feels natural.

Finally, hang the collage up in the room where you spend the most time. If you aren't sure where to put it, hang it in your bedroom, so that it can inspire you and you can absorb the energy even as you sleep. And know that this energy will guide you in the clutter clearing to come.

NAME YOUR HOME

There is power in a name. When you name something, whether it's a child, pet, plant, car, or home, you have a deeper energetic connection to it. Naming a home has been a common practice in many native cultures throughout the world, representing the belief that there is a consciousness within each home that serves as an unseen guardian for the people who reside in the home.

A name is more than a word—it honors the spirit of the being that carries that name.

To determine your home's name, go to the spot that feels like the heart of the home. If you aren't sure where that is, ask yourself where you feel the most love. When you are there, sit quietly, close your eyes, and allow yourself to imagine your home in human form, with a personality and an energy all its own. Then gently and lovingly ask the being that personifies your home for its name.

If you don't hear a word, but you experience a feeling, name the feeling. If you do hear a word, it may be unusual, even something you've never heard before. Or, it could be something traditional, like Sarah or Sam. Whatever you hear is perfect.

While you are in this meditative state, you can also ask your home what it needs for itself and the people it houses—this information can help guide your clutter-clearing sessions.

The more you address your home by its name, the more there is a positive, loving connection between you and your home, and the more your home can protect, nurture, and empower you.

QUESTIONS

What name did I hear for my home and how does my home support me and my dreams?

What did I notice about my home's personality?

_____
_____
_____
_____
_____
_____
_____
_____

What did my home tell me it needs?

_____
_____
_____
_____
_____
_____
_____
_____
_____

Clutter Clear Using a Bagua Energy Map

The *bagua* is a feng shui energy map that is overlaid over your home. It is one of the most powerful tools used in feng shui practices. It divides your space into nine separate areas—each one relating to a certain theme or aspect of your life. (See illustration.) Combined with clutter clearing, using a bagua map over your home can produce remarkable results.

How do I apply the bagua energy map over my home for my clutter clearing?

- Use an accurately scaled floor plan of your home (or room). It can also be a hand-drawn bird's-eye view of your home; have the dimensions as accurate as possible.

- Rotate the plan so the wall with the front door is at the bottom of your paper. The front door is the architecturally designed front door and not the door that you use all the time (if it is a different door).

- Overlay the three-by-three bagua grid, with the bottom of the grid aligned with the wall with the front door, such as in this illustration. (Make sure the grid is equally spaced.)

- In other words, the front door will open into one of three grid spaces. It will either open into the Knowledge and Self-Cultivation grid space, or the Career and Life Path grid, or the Helpful People, Angels, and Travel grid.

To use the bagua map for your clutter clearing, decide which area of your life you want to enhance, and clutter clear in that section. For example, if you want to release blockages to your prosperity, clutter clear in the far left section of your home with the intention that even more abundance flows into your life. For more information about using the bagua map, see my book *Feng Shui for the Soul*. Using the bagua map with your clearing can dramatically expand the results you get.

Bagua Energy Map

WEALTH & PROSPERITY	FAME & REPUTATION	LOVE & RELATIONSHIPS
FAMILY & COMMUNITY	HEALTH & WELL-BEING	CHILDREN & CREATIVITY
KNOWLEDGE & SELF-CULTIVATION	CAREER & LIFE PATH	HELPFUL PEOPLE & TRAVELS

FRONT OF HOUSE

Preparing for Your Clutter-Clearing Session

Before you begin the clearing process, make sure you have the supplies in place that will make it easy and efficient to move the items you're releasing from your home. They will include cleaning supplies, an open mind, and the following seven boxes:

1 The throwaway box is for items that have served their purpose and cannot be used by someone else.

2 The recycle box is for items that can be deposited in your recycle bin.

3 The donate box is for items that are still useful that you would like to pass along to a charity, group, or organization that can distribute these items for you.

4 The gift box is for items that you think a specific person or small group of people would enjoy. Take care not to burden someone else with your stuff—this box is only for items that someone you know would truly appreciate.

5 The sell box is for items that you no longer want but have monetary value—you can sell these things online, or to a consignment or pawn shop.

6 The maybe later box is for things that you aren't sure about or that you just don't feel quite ready to release. Once your clearing session is complete, seal this box up with tape, label it with a future date (six months or one year from now), and then give the box away if you haven't needed those items by that date.

7 The keep box may be your biggest box, as this is where you'll put the items you're keeping until your clutter-clearing session is finished, when you'll put them away.

Once you have your boxes, set some goals for your clearing journey. It might take more than one session. Clearing your home of clutter can take several sessions over a period of weeks or even months.

It can be emotionally and physically tiring, so allow yourself the time you need to make sure that you can be loving and intentional as you clear. Look at your schedule or calendar and decide how much time you can devote to clearing clutter and on what days.

QUESTIONS

What are my goals for clearing my clutter?

What days and times can I reserve for devoting to this process?

_____

_____

_____

_____

_____

_____

_____

_____

How will I reward myself or celebrate when this process is complete? (It's important to congratulate yourself at every step along the way.)

_____

_____

_____

_____

_____

_____

_____

_____

_____

_____

Beginning Your Clutter-Clearing Session

When you are ready to start a clutter-clearing session, choose an area to focus on, and then set a time for half the amount of time you have available. This way, you can empty and clear until the timer goes off, and then still have plenty of time to clean, organize, and put things away.

As you're deciding which box to place each item in, ask yourself:

- *Do I use this?*

- *Do I love it?*

- *Do I need it?*

- *Does this raise my energy, lower it, or keep it neutral?*

- *Does this fit who I am today, or who I want to become?*

- *Why am I keeping this? Who am I keeping it for?*

- *What will my life be like if I let it go?*

- *Will the freedom I gain by getting rid of this outweigh any possible regrets I may have about letting it go?*

If you answer yes to one or all of the first three questions, it goes right in the keep box.

If you answer these questions and are still having a hard time deciding which box it goes in, consider that clutter in one place may not be clutter in another. Is there perhaps another place in your home where this item would become useful, lovable, or necessary? When things are in their proper place they feel uplifting—not like clutter.

As you work, remember that clutter clearing is a sacred healing process, not a chore. It should feel like a spiritual adventure. So if you find that it starts to feel like an unpleasant task, stop! Reset. And start again when you are reenergized.

Make sure your clutter-clearing work feels joyous, which will yield more powerful results. You can make the process more meaningful by playing uplifting music, opening the windows (if the weather allows) to sweep out stagnant energy and allow fresh energy in, and perhaps running an essential oil diffuser or burning a candle or incense. Make it feel special and fun.

Even with all your preparation and planning, clutter clearing can at times feel overwhelming. It can seem like the energy in your home feels worse before it gets better. When you have your seven boxes out and the things you're keeping aren't fully put away yet, you might feel like, *My home may have been cluttered before, but now it feels like I have all this work to do to get to a new level of normal.* That is actually a great development, because as you stir up the contents and energy of your home, it's allowing the things that no longer serve you to come to the surface so you can release them. Take care of yourself and do what it takes to stay joyful and adventurous so that you can keep going and get to the point where only the good stuff remains.

CREATING A PERSONAL ALTAR FOR YOUR CLUTTER CLEARING

The desire to create sacred spaces is so deep in the human psyche that we often create them unconsciously. A gathering of personal objects on a deck or a gathering of photos on a piano can perhaps be an outer manifestation of an inner desire to establish hallowed spaces in our environment.

For thousands of years, people created altars in their dwellings. The home altar was a sacred space, a visible symbol of the connection between heaven and earth. It brought meaning into ordinary moments and served as a focal point for communing with spiritual realms. When you create an altar in conjunction with your clutter clearing, you magnify your results. And what could be a mundane act of clearing your clutter turns into a profound journey of the soul.

To create an altar to enhance your clutter clearing, consider the following:

1 Become clear on what new energy you want to bring into your home as a result of your clearing. (For example, you may want more love, more abundance, or more peace.)

2 Decide where you are going to set up your altar. If it is a temporary altar for your clearing, you may want to place it on a kitchen counter or a coffee table.

3 Discern what kind of objects serve as a metaphor for your desired results. For example, if you desire more peace, you might use a soothing color of blue for an altar cloth and place a ceramic dove or a Buddha in repose on your clutter-clearing altar to represent peace.

4 Take a moment to stand before this altar with a mindful heart focused on the task at hand with your clutter clearing.

5 When you are complete with your clearing, dismantle that altar with the same care that you used in creating it. (For more information, see my book *Altars: Bringing Sacred Shrines into Your Everyday Life*.)

part

II

CLUTTER CLEARING
ROOM BY ROOM

The Bedroom:
YOUR INNER SANCTUM

The bedroom is the space in your house that has the biggest influence on your energy, because it's where you replenish, renew, and dream. It's also where you go to heal and to deepen your connection to your beloved (if you are in a relationship). It is a reflection of your essential nature. When you walk into the bedroom, you want to feel as if you are being embraced. Your heart should open and your spirit should soar.

CLEARING CLUTTER

- Drawer by drawer, take everything out and then wipe down the inside of the drawer with a damp cloth.

- Decide what you no longer need, and then lovingly fold what you're keeping and replace it in the drawer.

- Clear off every surface and wipe it down with a damp cloth.

- For useful items that you need to keep, find a drawer or basket to store them in. Try to only keep beautiful or meaningful items on top of your bedside table, chest of drawers, and shelves.

- Remove everything from under your bed. Relocate (or give away) what you don't need regular access to. For anything that you have no other place to store, organize it neatly in under-the-bed storage containers.

DUMP, HONOR, FOLD

When clearing clutter from your drawers and shelves, use this three-part system:

1. Dump everything out, then clean the drawer.

2. Give thanks to each garment for protecting you from the elements and communicating who you are to the world.

3. Lovingly and neatly fold the garments you want to keep, and replace them in the drawer.

For added effect, play tranquil music and/or burn incense or light a candle while you do this. This process will help you infuse your garments with positive energy that you will activate when you wear the garment next.

ESSENTIAL OILS FOR THE BEDROOM

geranium, lavender, rose, ylang-ylang

FENG SHUI TIPS FOR THE BEDROOM

- The first thing you see in the morning and the last you see before you close your eyes at night should be something that uplifts you and inspires you to live the life you want.

- The art hanging on your bedroom walls should reflect qualities, people, places, or feelings that you desire. (If you are in a romantic relationship, think twice before displaying pictures of your children or parents, because it's the equivalent of inviting them into your bedroom.)

- Choose a sturdy yet welcoming headboard for your bed, and place the head of your bed against a wall so that you can feel supported.

- Keep exercise equipment and computers out of the bedroom—if that's not possible, hide them behind a screen or cover them with a large piece of cloth while you sleep.

- Resist the urge to store things under your bed as the energy of those things can disrupt your peaceful sleep.

- Invest in beautiful sheets—or iron the sheets that you have to infuse them with energy—to enhance the good feelings you experience when you crawl into bed.

OTHER PEOPLE'S BEDROOMS

Although it is tempting to clear the clutter of someone with whom you share a living space, such as a child or aging parent, it's important to remember that clutter to one person may be treasure to another, and the solution may lie in the fine art of compromise.

QUESTIONS

What is the very first thing I see when I open my eyes in the morning? How does what I see make me feel? If it reflected something about my life, what would it be? Can I change what I see first thing to something that reflects more of how I want to feel?

What items in my bedroom are not conducive to rest and relaxation? Can I move them or disguise them?

How can I clear the surfaces in this room so that there is more space?

_____

_____

_____

_____

_____

_____

_____

_____

What are some ways I can store the useful items I need to keep in the bedroom so that they are accessible, organized, and out of sight?

_____

_____

_____

_____

_____

_____

_____

_____

What beautiful and/or meaningful items can I display on my newly cleared surfaces?

What messages does the art that's hanging in my bedroom convey? Are these messages that promote replenishment?

How can I create a bedroom environment that is a metaphor for the future that I desire?

What are some ways I can deepen the rest I gain in my bedroom?

_____

_____

_____

_____

_____

_____

_____

_____

_____

_____

_____

_____

affirmations

"I am connected, supported, and safe."

"The more I restore myself, the more I can open my heart."

The Closet:
HOME OF YOUR IDENTITY

If you want to enhance or transform your life, clear the clutter out of your closet. Why? The clothes you wear not only reflect who you are but also send a message to yourself and to others about what matters to you and what you deserve in this life. They protect you from the elements and make you feel a certain way, whether it's sexy, comfortable, strong, or something else.

The closet should feel like a reflection of your best self, as it is where you choose how you will interact with the world. As you clear clutter from your closet, remember this: it's better to have a few outfits that make you feel stunning than a lot of outfits that make you feel just okay.

CLEARING CLUTTER

- Save de-cluttering your closet for a time when you have a full afternoon or even a full day or weekend, as it's more difficult to do this area piece by piece.

- Take everything out of your closet.

- Hold up each garment and ask, *Is this a reflection of who I am? Does it reflect who I desire to be? When I wear this, how do I feel? Do I love it? Do I use it? Does it fit? Does it look good on me? Does the color suit me? Does it need to be mended or cleaned?*

- Depending on your answer to these questions, place each item in the appropriate box.

- For the clothes you're keeping that you are hanging up, decide how you will organize them—by season, by color, by category (all the shirts, for example).

- For the clothes you are keeping that are stored on a shelf, nestle them in beautiful baskets.

ESSENTIAL OILS FOR THE CLOSET

cedarwood, eucalyptus, lavender, lemon, lemongrass, and rosemary

FENG SHUI TIPS FOR THE CLOSET

- The clothes stored in your closet should reflect who you are now or who you are growing into. Holding on to clothes that remind you of a less-than-joyous past will keep you stuck in the past. Releasing them will help free you up to fully arrive in the present.

- Organize your closet so that like items are stored together—it doesn't matter what system you use, only that you have a system.

- Keep your closet door closed when you're not using it. If you don't have a closet door, hang a curtain across the entrance that you can easily pull open and closed.

- Get rid of any items that make you feel bad—it doesn't matter if it's hidden in the closet, the energy will still affect you every time you go in the closet.

QUESTIONS

How does my closet feel overall? Is it cramped and crowded? Or open and uplifting?

What is the energy I feel when I stand in my closet and scan the clothes and possessions stored there?

If I could keep only eight outfits, what would they be and why? (Use the answer to this question to help you decide which clothes to keep and which you can release.)

_____

_____

_____

_____

_____

_____

_____

_____

_____

_____

_____

_____

_____

_____

affirmations

"I am comfortable in my own skin."

"My clothes protect me and reflect who I am at my core."

The Bathroom:
A REFUGE FOR RENEWAL

The bathroom is a place for releasing, relaxing, and adorning. It's a very intimate space where you can truly be yourself, releasing anything that you don't need. It's a place of cleansing and purification, and as such, you want it to feel clean and light—even a touch holy.

CLEARING CLUTTER

- As you move from cupboard to cupboard and drawer to drawer, take everything out.

- Wipe down the drawer with a damp cloth.

- Get rid of anything you no longer use, such as expired prescriptions and vitamins, old makeup, and shampoo or conditioner that you no longer use (you can transfer them to travel-sized bottles and use them in your toiletry bag if you can't bear to throw them out). If it feels right to you, you can even toss half-used cold medicines (keeping them around "in case I catch a cold" can be, for some people, an affirmation for getting sick).

- Only put items you'll use back in the drawer or on the shelf, using drawer organizers or baskets to keep them contained, easily accessible, and pretty. Wipe each item off with a damp cloth before you replace it.

- Clear as much as possible off the counters and find a place for them in a drawer, on a shelf, or in a cabinet.

- Look for ways to create beauty—storing your Epsom salts in a glass jar with a ribbon tied around it, for example, and replacing your frayed towels with beautiful new ones that you fold nicely so that they look even better.

- If you share the bathroom with someone who isn't as committed to clearing clutter as you are, divide the space so that you each have a personal area—and then focus on making your space as clear as it can be, letting them do as they wish with their area. (Try to come to an agreement about the counter, as a clutter-free counter is important for the overall energy of the room.)

ESSENTIAL OILS FOR THE BATHROOM

eucalyptus, fir, lemon, lime, peppermint, rose, ylang-ylang

FENG SHUI TIPS FOR THE BATHROOM

- Keep the lid to the toilet closed so that the energy in the room doesn't immediately and symbolically "go down the drain."

- Put a plant on the back of the toilet, whether it's real or artificial, to replenish any energy that may get symbolically flushed away.

- Hang a beautiful picture above the toilet to draw your attention upward.

- Make sure the mirror in your bathroom stays clean, is clear, and makes you look great.

- Keep a stopper in your drains to symbolically prevent energy from being washed away.

QUESTIONS

How does the bathroom feel overall?

How do I feel when I am in the bathroom?

_____

_____

_____

_____

_____

_____

_____

_____

What can I do to enhance the energy of renewal in this room?

_____

_____

_____

_____

_____

_____

_____

_____

_____

_____

How can I create more beauty in this room?

affirmations

"I release what no longer serves."

"I renew myself every morning and every night."

The Entryway:
A PORTAL BETWEEN YOUR INNER AND OUTER WORLDS

The entrance to your home is where energy flows into and out of your home. From a feng shui perspective, it is a metaphor for your life, and as such, you want it to be functional, beautiful, and clutter free. The more welcoming your entryway, the more good energy will flow into your life.

CLEARING CLUTTER

- If there is a closet or coatrack in your front hall, treat it the same way you did your bedroom closet—take everything down, assess everything piece by piece, wipe down any shelves, vacuum the floor, and only put back what you love and use.

- Take up everything off the floor and vacuum, then wash the floor. If you kick off your shoes as soon as you come home, find a shoe storage system so that every pair has a place to go.

- Place something beautiful or inspiring that you can see as soon as you walk in the front door.

- Find an attractive way to contain your mail, keys, and other items that you need to have close to the front door. When everything has a place to return to, you won't have to spend time searching for—and stressing over—misplaced items.

ESSENTIAL OILS FOR THE ENTRYWAY

bergamot, cedarwood, fir, lemon, neroli, orange, pine, sage, sandalwood, vetiver

FENG SHUI TIPS FOR THE ENTRYWAY

- Make sure your entry is well lit, with a clear path from the street (or hallway, if you live in an apartment) to your door.

- Ensure that your front door opens and closes smoothly— no creaking, no piles on the floor that prevent it from opening fully.

- Put something beautiful on either side of your front door. If there are small windows alongside or in your door, keep them sparkling clean.

QUESTIONS

If a stranger were to stand at my front door, what kind of decisions or judgments would they make about me based on the energy of the door and the immediate entryway?

What can I see as soon as I walk in my front door? What does this view say about me and my life? Is there something more uplifting I could place there?

What might I need to do (or what actions step would I need to take)
to feel as I desire in my entryway?

What is my time line for these action steps? Make your list as specific as you can.

------

affirmations

"I am at home."

"I welcome the good radiant life force into my life."

The Kitchen:
SEAT OF ABUNDANCE

The kitchen is where you nourish yourself and your loved ones. It's where you gather, and where you transform the abundant raw materials that nature provides into sustenance. As such, it also symbolizes financial resources, as money is another way that we sustain ourselves.

The underlying energy of the kitchen is to bring more vitality and prosperity into your life. It's also the workhorse of the house, so you want it to easily support you in the work of feeding yourself and others, and it requires the most daily maintenance to keep it functioning and energized.

CLEARING CLUTTER

- Decide where you will start—drawers or cabinets? Begin wherever you feel most drawn.

- Whether it's a drawer or a cabinet, take everything out. Clean the empty drawer or shelf with a damp cloth.

- For every item of food, check the expiration date and throw out anything that is long past it. Ask yourself, *Will I eat this? Will my family eat it?* For every utensil, ask, *Do I use this? Do I need to keep it?*

- Only put back the items that you know you will use. Store like things with like things (snacks together, canned goods together). Arrange them artfully so that when you open the cabinet or drawer, you get a little zing of exhilaration.

- Clear off your counters as much as possible. Store small appliances out of sight, hang utensils from a wall-mounted rack instead of keeping them on a counter. Store things that you need easy access to (such as vitamins) in a beautiful basket.

- Tidy up any magnets and photos on your refrigerator. You don't need to take everything down, but make sure these items uplift you when you look at them rather than appearing chaotic.

- Pull out all the cleaning supplies from under the sink and evaluate what you truly need to keep. Store the supplies in a plastic bin or in drawers that you can easily access.

ESSENTIAL OILS FOR THE KITCHEN

lemon, lemongrass, grapefruit, peppermint

FENG SHUI TIPS FOR THE KITCHEN

- Repair or get rid of any appliances that don't work, or don't work properly. From a feng shui perspective, the energy of broken appliances can impede your ability to sustain and provide for yourself and your family.

- Your stove represents abundance—make sure all the burners are working, and take care to use all the burners on your stove so that your abundance is firing on all cylinders. Keep the stovetop clean. Although it can be a personal preference, in traditional feng shui it is beneficial to not store any empty pans on the stove (or at least put a lid on them). The idea is that pans represent abundance, and empty pans represent empty prosperity.

- As much as you can, make sure the kitchen is clean at night before you go to bed—sink clear, counters wiped, everything put away—as it will help you start each day with refreshed energy.

- The plumbing in your kitchen and throughout your home correlates to emotions, so tend to any clogged drains or leaking faucets. Traditionally, water in the home represents emotions—clogged water can represent clogged emotions, stagnant water can represent stagnant emotions, dripping water can symbolize uncontained emotions, and so on.

- Pots of herbs growing on the windowsill, wreaths of garlic or dried chile peppers, a pretty jar filled with tea all represent the abundance of nature and are great items to have on display.

- Choose a functional trash can and keep it clean—the more attractive and clean your trash can is, the better the energy will be in your kitchen.

QUESTIONS

What is the current energy in the kitchen? When I stand in it and close my eyes, how do I feel?

_____

_____

_____

_____

_____

_____

_____

What might a stranger think about a person who has a kitchen like this?

_____

_____

_____

_____

_____

_____

_____

_____

_____

How do I desire to feel in the kitchen?

_____

_____

_____

_____

_____

_____

_____

What action steps would I need to take to feel as I desire in
my kitchen?

_____

_____

_____

_____

_____

_____

_____

_____

_____

What is my time line for these action steps?

_____

_____

_____

_____

_____

_____

_____

_____

_____

_____

_____

affirmation

"As I prepare food and use my kitchen, I'm bringing more vitality,
health, and prosperity to myself and my family."

The Dining Room:

GATHERING PLACE FOR MULTIPLE KINDS OF NOURISHMENT

Whether you have a formal dining room or a dining table in an alcove off the living room or kitchen, the dining area is where we come together with the people we love—or even just ourselves—to eat the food and nurture the relationships that sustain us. It is symbolic of supportive, enjoyable, and loving relationships. The energy of the dining area is so powerful that it extends beyond the walls of your home to inform your relationships to people who may never set foot inside your home.

CLEARING CLUTTER

- Commonplace objects such as the mail, your purse and keys, or paperwork often end up on the dining table. As a suggestion, find another place for them (as ideally your dining table should be clear) or make sure they are neat and organized, perhaps in a special basket.

- The dining table can be a great place for projects, such as a puzzle or arts and crafts endeavors. However, make sure you are continually working on those projects, rather than letting them "go to seed" on your table.

- If you store napkins, glasses, candles, or other linens in this room, make sure they are beautifully arranged in baskets or nicely organized in a drawer or inside a cabinet so there isn't visual clutter.

ESSENTIAL OILS FOR THE DINING ROOM

bergamot, peppermint, sweet orange

FENG SHUI TIPS FOR THE DINING ROOM

- Place a bowl of fruit or a vase of flowers in the middle of your table to represent and invite abundance.

- Ideally keep TVs, clocks, and other electronic appliances that make you conscious of time passing out of the dining room. You want the energy here to feel timeless, so that you are encouraged to linger and enjoy the bonds that eating together creates.

QUESTIONS

How can I clear the surfaces in this room so there is more space for connection and communion with the people I love?

What bowls or vases can I use to display fruits and flowers in the middle of our table and invite in more abundance?

If a stranger were to look at my dining area, what kinds of assumptions would they make about the people who eat at this table?

How do I desire to feel in the dining room?

What action steps would I need to take to feel as I desire in my dining room?

_____

_____

_____

_____

_____

_____

What is my time line for these action steps?

_____

_____

_____

_____

_____

_____

affirmations

"I have more than enough to sustain myself,
my family, and my friends."

"My life is enjoyable and good for me."

The Living Room:
HUB OF THE HOME

The living room is where we gather with friends and family—where we communicate and enjoy each other's company. It's also where we go to relax. You want to feel at ease, supported, and safe when you are in the living room. You want the overall feel of the living room to be welcoming—cozy blankets (if you live in a cold climate), comfortable places to sit, pleasing art, plants or a view to look at, and activities to do together.

CLEARING CLUTTER

- Contain any cords around the TV or stereo. If you have a large collection of CDs, records, or DVDs, but you don't watch or listen to them regularly, move them somewhere else (maybe you can give some away, or store them in a basket or attractive box in a closet).

- Clear everything off the mantel, wipe it down, and then only replace the items that you love. Arrange them artfully.

- If you have bookshelves in your room, ask yourself if you will really ever look at or read the books you have there, or if the title or genre is something that makes you feel good or feel bad. Take down all the books, assess them one by one, and only keep the ones you love. For those books you keep, arrange them so that they are visually compelling—perhaps by color or size, or by interspersing them with photos, vases, or other objects that you love and that transmit the energy or feeling that you want in your life.

ESSENTIAL OILS FOR THE LIVING ROOM

bergamot, juniper, orange, pine

FENG SHUI TIPS FOR THE LIVING ROOM

- Changing the color in your living room—painting one wall, or bringing in new pillows or curtains—is a quick way to change the energy in your living room.

- Moving furniture around is also an energy uplifter. Whatever arrangement makes you feel like *That's it!* is great. Whatever feels good is good feng shui.

- This is a great place to display photos of family—especially pictures that show you enjoying each other's company and having fun.

QUESTIONS

If there were one word to describe the underlying energy in my living room, what would it be and why?

_____

_____

_____

_____

_____

_____

_____

_____

When I stand in the living room and close my eyes, how do I feel?

_____

_____

_____

_____

_____

_____

_____

_____

_____

_____

What might a stranger think about a person who has a living room like this?

How do I desire to feel in the living room?

What action steps would I need to take to feel as I desire in my living room?

What is my time line for these action steps?

_____

_____

_____

_____

_____

_____

_____

_____

_____

_____

_____

affirmations

"I relax."

"I have excellent relationships with my friends and family."

The Home Office:

SEAT OF CREATIVITY AND SUCCESS

The office is the place of productivity and creativity. If you perform work that produces your income in your home office, you may want to clutter clear it first, because the energy of your home office influences all the work you do there. It should be a place that gives you joy and makes you feel competent. The more at ease you are in this space, and the more it is set up to support you in your efforts, the more your productivity and abundance will flow.

CLEARING CLUTTER

- Most of the things we store in files we never look at again. Go through your files and let go of anything you do not use and do not need. If there is something you need to keep—such as the last seven years of tax returns—put it in a box that you label and store in a closet or the basement. Instruction manuals for appliances can generally be found online—recycle the paper versions.

- Devote some time to reducing computer clutter. Go through your digital files and delete whatever you have not used. If there's a file you think you might need to access some day, upload it to the cloud or to an external hard drive or flash drive, and then put that drive in a safe place. Also, go through your contacts, and if there are people you don't know or don't like, clear them out so that their energy is no longer in your computer. If your desktop is cluttered, make folders to organize those documents, and then put all of those folders in one desktop folder so that you have a beautiful, clear space on your computer screen.

- Make sure your chair is comfortable and supports your body as you work.

- Organize your computer cords with little Velcro strips that can bundle them together, and then label them.

- Clear off all the surfaces, giving all papers, pens, files, notebooks, and books a home. Throw out the pens that don't work—it's better to only have a few pens you love than a whole container full of pens that don't write well.

- Wipe down the surfaces of your desk, keyboard, and computer screen.

- Place only beautiful things on your desk.

ESSENTIAL OILS FOR THE HOME OFFICE

basil, bergamot, peppermint, rosemary

- You want everything in your office to propel you toward excellence, creativity, and joy.

- The objects you keep around your computer are a subliminal altar. Make sure these things uplift your energy.

- Arrange your desk so that you can see the door to the room when you are sitting at it.

- The far left corner of your desk in feng shui is associated with wealth. Put something that represents abundance in that far left-hand corner, such as a small bowl that holds items that signify wealth to you.

QUESTIONS

Why do I want to clear this space?

_____

_____

_____

_____

_____

_____

_____

_____

_____

_____

What results do I want to create by clearing the clutter from this space?

How do I wish to feel in this space?

What items can I get rid of that are no longer serving me?

_____

_____

_____

_____

_____

_____

_____

_____

What emotions or memories did I experience while clearing this room?

_____

_____

_____

_____

_____

_____

_____

_____

_____

_____

_____

What did I accomplish during my clearing?

_____

_____

_____

_____

_____

_____

_____

_____

_____

_____

_____

_____

affirmations

"I love my work."

"All that I do produces excellent results."

"Abundance is flowing into my life."

The Attic and Basement:

PAST AND FUTURE

It's not just the spaces that you see every day that you want to clear—the attic and basement are also important areas of your home, and the energy of the items you store there has a big impact on you and anyone who lives in the home with you. The attic represents your higher aspirations. It is generally full of things that are from the past, and if it is overstuffed and chaotic, it can make you feel like you continually have things hanging over your head that are preventing you from moving forward.

The basement represents your foundation, and it can house an energy of things being hidden under the surface—whether they are desires you are suppressing or issues related to the past. So if you want to heal old wounds and bring forth more of what you truly want in life, de-cluttering your basement is an important part of the process.

CLEARING CLUTTER

- For anything you aren't sure about, put it in a box and label it "Don't open until" and write a date that is one year from now. If you haven't opened it in a year, take it straight to the thrift store.

- For the items you're keeping, use beautiful storage containers and label them clearly.

- Install sturdy shelving to organize those containers.

- Make sure any tools, furniture, or appliances that are stored in these areas are in good working order. If you can't use it, and can't get it repaired, it is time to let it go.

ESSENTIAL OILS FOR THE ATTIC AND BASEMENT

lemongrass, orange, pine, rose, sage

FENG SHUI TIPS FOR THE ATTIC AND BASEMENT

- Clean out any mold and dust, which represent stagnant energy.

- Make sure the lighting is bright so that you can bring whatever you store there into the light.

- Create clear paths for walking through these spaces—you want energy to move freely here.

- It can be tiring to sort through items from your past because of the emotions and memories they bring up. Play uplifting music, spritz essential oils, and burn a candle to make the experience more intentional and more supportive.

QUESTIONS

What issues do the contents of my attic and/or basement represent?

_____

_____

_____

_____

_____

_____

_____

_____

How can I lighten my energy by clearing these spaces?

_____

_____

_____

_____

_____

_____

_____

_____

_____

_____

How can I use these spaces in a productive way?

What memories or emotions do I experience as I clear the clutter from these areas?

What action steps do I need to take in order to clear these spaces?

What is the time line for these action steps? What support do I need?

affirmations

"My foundations are strong."

"I am open, clear, and free."

The Garage:
PLACE OF PROTECTION

The garage is typically the most cluttered space in the home environment. It's generally where we stick things that have no other place to go. Having a jumbled mess of items means that the garage can't adequately do its primary job, which is to protect your car and your belongings. Your garage can be a place of beauty and grace, a space that makes you feel safe and supported. It is often dirty work, but playing music can make it fun. And it will feel so amazing to have a beautifully organized garage.

CLEARING CLUTTER

- Devote a full day or even a weekend to clearing out the garage, because just as with every other space, you want to pull everything out of it. You may need to enlist the help of friends or someone you pay to help move things around.

- Use shelving, storage containers, and hooks to give every-thing a home.

- Aim for beauty as well as organization—perhaps paint a wall.

- Only keep what you love and what you will use. Release everything else.

ESSENTIAL OILS FOR THE GARAGE

eucalyptus, fir, frankincense, lemongrass, myrrh, sage, sandalwood

FENG SHUI TIPS FOR THE GARAGE

- If you are using the garage to store your car, it is the first thing you see when you arrive home and the last thing you see before you head out into the world. Seek to make it feel welcoming and protective. Hang a poster or other artwork that you can see from the front seat.

- If there is a bedroom above your garage, it is extra import-ant to clear the clutter from the garage, as the energy of the things stored there will radiate upward into the bedroom.

QUESTIONS

What is the overall feeling in the garage?

What would a stranger who walked into my garage think about me based on the energy in this space?

What is the first thing I see when I pull my car into the garage, and how can I make this view more uplifting?

_____

_____

_____

_____

_____

_____

_____

What action steps do I need to take in order to clear my garage?

_____

_____

_____

_____

_____

_____

_____

_____

_____

What is the time line for these action steps? What support do I need?

---

affirmations

"I am safe and protected."

"All is well in my life."

The Car:
FREEDOM AND IDENTITY

This is one area that people often don't think about when they're clutter clearing, but it's very important. Our cars are reflections of our identity—if they weren't, we'd all drive the same kind of car. People buy the kind of cars that reflect who they believe they are, or who they'd like to be. Your car also represents freedom, because it can take you wherever you need to go. By clearing the clutter and raising the energy in your car, you can experience and convey a deeper sense of who you are in the world.

CLEARING CLUTTER

- Take everything out of the car—the items in the glove box, the console, the trunk, the pockets on the back of the seat, on the floor mats, and everything that's gotten trapped underneath the seats.

- Wipe down and vacuum every surface that you can.

- If you don't already have one, get a trash bin for your car so that any future messes are contained—then, every time you get gas or charge your car, you can easily empty the trash.

- You might also consider getting an essential oil diffuser that is designed to plug into the USB port in your car, or hanging something beautiful and meaningful from your rearview mirror—whatever makes your car feel like a sanctuary.

ESSENTIAL OILS FOR THE CAR

lavender, rosemary, sandalwood, spearmint, thyme, vetiver

FENG SHUI TIPS FOR THE CAR

- Give your car a name if you haven't already—anything that has a name performs better.

- Place an item for protection in your car—perhaps a figurine of your favorite religious figure or superhero, or a crystal that you keep in your console or glove compartment.

- Consider getting an essential oil diffuser that plugs into the cigarette lighter to continually clear and uplift the energy in your car.

QUESTIONS

If a stranger were to climb into my car, what assumptions would they make about me?

_____

_____

_____

_____

_____

_____

_____

How do I desire to feel when I am in my car?

_____

_____

_____

_____

_____

_____

_____

_____

What changes can I make to my car that will make all my journeys more joyous?

What name fits my car and why?

Where do I want to go in this life—physically and metaphorically—
and how can the symbolic energy of my car help me get there?

_____

_____

_____

_____

_____

_____

_____

_____

_____

_____

_____

_____

_____

_____

_____

_____

_____

_____

_____

_____

_____

_____

_____

_____

_____

_____

_____

_____

_____

_____

_____

_____

_____

_____

_____

affirmation

"All my journeys in life are joyous."

Completing the Cycle: Space Clearing after Clutter Clearing

Have you ever walked into an empty room and immediately sensed the atmosphere was laced with tension? You may have had no idea what had occurred there prior to your arrival, yet you somehow knew it was something unpleasant. By contrast, another place you entered gave you a feeling of joy and well-being for no apparent reason. The differences between rooms that feel great and ones that seem depressing can be explained, at least in part, by the energy within that space.

Your clutter clearing will, of course, make your home feel much lighter. However, to deepen the flow of beneficial energy, you may want to consider completing your clutter clearing with a space clearing. Space clearing is an ancient art form that has recently been finding popularity . . . for the simple reason that it works. After a space is cleared, the positive feeling in the space is palpable.

Here are five steps you can take to uplift the energy in your home after your clutter clearing:

1 Decide what kind of energy you want to flow through your home. (For example, do you want joy, love, peace, abundance, or creativity?)

2 Choose a tool for your space clearing. (The tools are less important than your intent and your prayers.) Traditional items like bells, gongs, drums, rattles, salt, or smoldering herbs are often used for space clearing.

3 In many cultures there is the belief that sound breaks up stagnant energy, so if you decide to use something like a bell for your clearing, stand at the entrance to each room, and hold the bell to your heart while focusing on your overall intent for your home. Then slowly ring the bell while you walk clockwise around each room. You can use this circling method with any space-clearing tool you choose.

4 At the conclusion of each room, take your bell to make a figure eight, to symbolically seal the beneficial energy into that space.

5 When you have completed the space clearing, you will feel an enormous difference in your home's energy. For more information about space clearing, see my books *Sacred Space* and *The Secrets of Space Clearing*.

part

CLUTTER CLEARING
FOR YOUR LIFE

Time:

THE CONTAINER
FOR YOUR LIFE

Clutter is not just about stuff. In our modern society, despite all our time-saving devices, our time is cluttered too with obligations, distractions, and things that don't feed our souls.

The truth is, we all have a limited amount of time to be alive. Now is the perfect time to begin making more conscious decisions about how you want to spend your precious time. As you clutter clear your time, you will more easily be able to move toward your desired dreams and goals.

CLEARING CLUTTER

- Make two pie charts. In the first, draw the breakdown of how you are currently spending your time—what percentages of your daily 24 hours are you spending sleeping, eating and preparing food, taking care of yourself, working, using your computer, watching TV, using your phone, exercising, volunteering or helping others, spending time with family or friends, or doing hobbies?

- In the second, draw how you would like your day to be broken up.

- Looking at your two charts, ask yourself which activities you could do less of or release altogether and what activities you could do more of.

QUESTIONS

Given that I have a limited amount of time remaining in my life, what is it I want to experience? How do I want to cherish this time?

_____

_____

_____

_____

_____

_____

_____

_____

Looking at my pie chart of how I spend my time, which activities light me up, and which ones drain me?

_____

_____

_____

_____

_____

_____

_____

_____

Remembering that I only have a limited amount of time left in life, is there anything that I could do less of (or more of) that could empower my life?

_____

_____

_____

_____

_____

_____

_____

_____

What could I shift that could move me more in the direction of my desired use of time?

_____

_____

_____

_____

_____

_____

_____

_____

How do I want to spend my time once I clear some of my time clutter?

What is the best thing that I can do if I clear and create more time in my life?

_____

_____

_____

_____

_____

_____

_____

_____

_____

_____

_____

_____

_____

affirmation

"There is enough time to experience everything
I want to experience in this life."

Guided Visualization: Creating a Home That Serves Your Purpose

Allow yourself several minutes to lie or sit somewhere you can completely relax and breathe freely. Imagine yourself to be in the most restorative place on earth for you—maybe it's a cabin in the snow, a country cottage, a crystal palace, or a beautiful forest. You may need to ask these questions several times as these answers can take years or even a lifetime to fully emerge. By simply asking these questions, the answers will begin to surface. They may appear in signs and symbols that spontaneously materialize around you. The answers may come forth in a dream. There is a place inside you that knows the answers, and becoming aware of your answers will help you make decisions about how you want to spend your time— and who you want to spend it with.

Who am I, really?

_____

_____

_____

_____

_____

_____

_____

_____

_____

What is my purpose?

If a stranger were to look at everything that has happened in my life up until now, what would they say my purpose is?

If I'm not sure of my purpose, what might help me figure it out? If I would like to change my purpose, what would it be?

_____

_____

_____

_____

_____

_____

_____

What do I most value in life?

_____

_____

_____

_____

_____

_____

_____

_____

_____

What would my ideal home—one that reflects my purpose and values—feel like? What would it look like?

_____

_____

_____

_____

_____

_____

_____

How can I make my current home more closely match my ideal home?

_____

_____

_____

_____

_____

_____

_____

_____

_____

Relationships:
OUR MOST IMPORTANT TEACHERS

One of the major ways we learn important lessons in life is through our relationships. The people you spend the most time with have enormous influence over your life. As such, if your relationships do not uplift you, feel supportive, or help you move toward your destiny, they can be cluttering up your energy field.

As you consider the relationships in your life, remember that it's better to have one or two good, strong relationships than a whole lot of people who don't support you or believe in you.

CLEARING RELATIONSHIP CLUTTER

- Take an objective look at the items in your home—which ones remind you of a relationship that drags your energy down? Or keeps you stuck in the past? Or triggers negative energy or emotions when you look at them?

- Start taking note of how you feel when you are with certain people, as well as how you feel after you've spent time with them. Let this information guide your choices on whom you spend your time with.

- Start to proactively reach out to people whose energy lights you up—spending more time with people who are an energetic match for you and your desires will naturally diminish the time you have to spend with people who aren't.

QUESTIONS

Who do I spend the most time with?

_____

_____

_____

_____

_____

_____

_____

_____

Which relationships raise my energy?

_____

_____

_____

_____

_____

_____

_____

_____

_____

_____

Which relationships lower my energy?

Which relationships have a neutral impact on my energy?

When I close my eyes and envision a relationship with a person who opens my heart and feeds my soul, what do I see and feel?

_____

_____

_____

_____

_____

_____

_____

Are there any items in my home that have negative energy from a past or current relationship? Can I let these things go?

_____

_____

_____

_____

_____

_____

_____

_____

_____

For the people in my life who don't feed my energy, but I can't or don't want to cut ties with them, what steps can I take to protect my energy when I am with them?

affirmation

"More and more, I am surrounded by relationships
that are nurturing and loving."

Thoughts:
CREATING NEW PATHWAYS

Perhaps one of the most insidious kinds of clutter can occur within your thoughts. Many of us have so many thoughts bouncing around our minds at all times that there is no space for stillness. This makes it hard to have clarity on your life—on the items, experiences, commitments, and relationships that either lift you up or deplete you. It also makes it feel like your life is whizzing by—life becomes longer when you are able to experience what is happening in the moment rather than have your attention hooked by your passing thoughts.

There is also incredible power in the words you tell yourself—whatever your thoughts say, you tend to believe. So it's well worth your time to practice letting go of negative thoughts and actively training your brain to focus on positive thoughts. The more you clear out thought patterns that do not serve you, the more you clear the pathway to what you want.

The first step to clutter clearing your thoughts is awareness of them. The second step is knowing that you can change them. The past does not need to equal the future.

CLEARING CLUTTER

- Start by deciding to sit still for one minute. During this minute, don't encourage or deny your thoughts. Simply notice them. Allow them to be like clouds drifting across the sky—you can identify that they are there and then let them keep passing by.

- Commit to sitting in stillness, simply noticing your thoughts, for one minute per day. When you are ready for more, you can do one minute of stillness two, three, or even four times during the day.

- A helpful trick to reframe your thoughts is this: Instead of asking yourself why you did something, or why something happened, ask yourself a question that starts with *how* instead. *How can I do this differently next time? How can I notice that I'm upset? When I do notice that I'm upset, how can I make myself feel better?*

- If you catch yourself saying a negative thought about yourself, just say to yourself, *Cancel, cancel.*

- Challenge yourself to find something good about everything you experience. As you find the good, you help bring it into existence.

QUESTIONS

How often, and when, do I think negative thoughts about myself during a typical day? How can I shift that energy?

How often do I assign meaning to my actions, or others' actions, that are not empowering? (For example, how often do you make a mistake and think something like *I am so stupid. Of course I messed that up. I'm never going to get this?*)

Is my general view of the future negative or positive?

How much time do I spend revisiting the past and does it empower me? Why?

_____

_____

_____

_____

_____

_____

_____

How much time do I spend worrying about the future and does it empower me? Why?

_____

_____

_____

_____

_____

_____

_____

_____

How often, and when, do I say negative things to myself and others? What do I gain from this?

_____

_____

_____

_____

_____

_____

When someone else is talking, how much am I listening to them, and how much am I thinking instead about what I'll say in response?

_____

_____

_____

_____

_____

_____

affirmations

"The thoughts I think influence my reality."

"I choose to focus on the good."

The Journey
Is the Reward

Perhaps one of the most insidious kinds of clutter
can occur within your thoughts. Many of us have
so many thoughts bouncing around our minds at all
times that there is no space for stillness. This makes
it hard to have clarity on your life—on the items,
experiences, commitments, and relationships that
either lift you up or deplete you. It also makes it
feel like your life is whizzing by—life becomes longer
when you are able to experience what is happening in the moment rather than have your attention
hooked by your passing thoughts.

There is also incredible power in the words you
tell yourself—whatever your thoughts say, you tend to
believe. So it's well worth your time to practice letting
go of negative thoughts and actively training your
brain to focus on positive thoughts. The more you
clear out thought patterns that do not serve you, the
more you clear the pathway to what you want.

The first step to clutter clearing your thoughts
is awareness of them. The second step is knowing
that you can change them. The past does not need
to equal the future.

QUESTIONS

What did my efforts to clear my clutter teach me?

What strategies can I use to minimize the future accumulation of clutter in my home?

What strategies can I use to minimize the future accumulation of clutter in my time?

What strategies can I use to minimize the future accumulation of clutter in my relationships?

What strategies can I use to minimize the future accumulation of clutter in my thoughts?

What results have I already seen from my efforts?

Who or what do I want to thank for helping me along the way?

What do I want to make sure I remember the next time I need to do another round of clutter clearing?

_____

_____

_____

_____

_____

_____

_____

How am I going to celebrate my clutter-clearing success?

_____

_____

_____

_____

_____

_____

_____

_____

_____

_____

14-Day

CLUTTER-CLEARING
JOURNEY

The following pages will offer you a day-
by-day section to keep track of your
clutter-clearing results for two weeks.

Example Entry

My overall intent for this sacred clutter-clearing journey is . . .

To gain clarity about my purpose in life.

My intent for today's clearing is . . .

To feel good about myself and my
life choices.

My desired physical results for today's journey are . . .

To clean all the drawers in the bedroom.

My desired emotional results for today's journey are . . .

To feel relaxed and at ease no matter
what is occurring around me.

Here's what I accomplished today . . .

I completed clearing almost all of my
bedroom drawers.

Here is what I felt today . . .

Somehow I felt sad as I went through my
drawers. I had a forgotten memory of my
grandmother helping me clean my bedroom as
a young girl. My grandmother always seemed
to understand me when no one else did.

Here is what I'm doing to celebrate my results . . .

To celebrate I'm going to sit outside with
a glass of iced tea and do absolutely
nothing but look at the clouds. It feels so
good to do this.

Day 1

DATE:

My overall intent for this sacred clutter-clearing journey is . . .

_____

_____

_____

_____

My intent for today's clearing is . . .

_____

_____

_____

_____

My desired physical results for today's journey are . . .

_____

_____

_____

My desired emotional results for today's journey are . . .

_____

_____

_____

_____

Here's what I accomplished today . . .

Here is what I felt today . . .

Here is what I'm doing to celebrate my results . . .

Day 2

My overall intent for this sacred clutter-clearing journey is . . .

_____

_____

_____

_____

My intent for today's clearing is . . .

_____

_____

_____

_____

My desired physical results for today's journey are . . .

_____

_____

_____

_____

My desired emotional results for today's journey are . . .

_____

_____

_____

_____

Here's what I accomplished today . . .

Here is what I felt today . . .

Here is what I'm doing to celebrate my results . . .

Day 3

My overall intent for this sacred clutter-clearing journey is . . .

_____

_____

_____

_____

My intent for today's clearing is . . .

_____

_____

_____

_____

My desired physical results for today's journey are . . .

_____

_____

_____

My desired emotional results for today's journey are . . .

_____

_____

_____

_____

Here's what I accomplished today . . .

_____

_____

_____

_____

_____

Here is what I felt today . . .

_____

_____

_____

_____

_____

Here is what I'm doing to celebrate my results . . .

_____

_____

_____

_____

_____

_____

Day 4

My overall intent for this sacred clutter-clearing journey is . . .

_____

_____

_____

_____

My intent for today's clearing is . . .

_____

_____

_____

_____

My desired physical results for today's journey are . . .

_____

_____

_____

My desired emotional results for today's journey are . . .

_____

_____

_____

_____

Here's what I accomplished today . . .

Here is what I felt today . . .

Here is what I'm doing to celebrate my results . . .

Day 5

DATE:

My overall intent for this sacred clutter-clearing journey is . . .

My intent for today's clearing is . . .

My desired physical results for today's journey are . . .

My desired emotional results for today's journey are . . .

Here's what I accomplished today . . .

Here is what I felt today . . .

Here is what I'm doing to celebrate my results . . .

Day 6

My overall intent for this sacred clutter-clearing journey is . . .

My intent for today's clearing is . . .

My desired physical results for today's journey are . . .

My desired emotional results for today's journey are . . .

Here's what I accomplished today . . .

Here is what I felt today . . .

Here is what I'm doing to celebrate my results . . .

Day 7

DATE:

My overall intent for this sacred clutter-clearing journey is . . .

My intent for today's clearing is . . .

My desired physical results for today's journey are . . .

My desired emotional results for today's journey are . . .

Here's what I accomplished today . . .

_____

_____

_____

_____

_____

Here is what I felt today . . .

_____

_____

_____

_____

_____

Here is what I'm doing to celebrate my results . . .

_____

_____

_____

_____

_____

_____

Day 8

My overall intent for this sacred clutter-clearing journey is . . .

_____

_____

_____

_____

My intent for today's clearing is . . .

_____

_____

_____

My desired physical results for today's journey are . . .

_____

_____

_____

My desired emotional results for today's journey are . . .

_____

_____

_____

_____

Here's what I accomplished today . . .

Here is what I felt today . . .

Here is what I'm doing to celebrate my results . . .

Day 9

My overall intent for this sacred clutter-clearing journey is . . .

My intent for today's clearing is . . .

My desired physical results for today's journey are . . .

My desired emotional results for today's journey are . . .

Here's what I accomplished today . . .

Here is what I felt today . . .

Here is what I'm doing to celebrate my results . . .

Day 10

My overall intent for this sacred clutter-clearing journey is . . .

My intent for today's clearing is . . .

My desired physical results for today's journey are . . .

My desired emotional results for today's journey are . . .

Here's what I accomplished today . . .

Here is what I felt today . . .

Here is what I'm doing to celebrate my results . . .

Day 11

DATE:

My overall intent for this sacred clutter-clearing journey is . . .

My intent for today's clearing is . . .

My desired physical results for today's journey are . . .

My desired emotional results for today's journey are . . .

Here's what I accomplished today . . .

Here is what I felt today . . .

Here is what I'm doing to celebrate my results . . .

Day 12

My overall intent for this sacred clutter-clearing journey is . . .

My intent for today's clearing is . . .

My desired physical results for today's journey are . . .

My desired emotional results for today's journey are . . .

Here's what I accomplished today . . .

Here is what I felt today . . .

Here is what I'm doing to celebrate my results . . .

Day 13

My overall intent for this sacred clutter-clearing journey is . . .

_____

_____

_____

_____

My intent for today's clearing is . . .

_____

_____

_____

_____

My desired physical results for today's journey are . . .

_____

_____

_____

My desired emotional results for today's journey are . . .

_____

_____

_____

_____

Here's what I accomplished today . . .

Here is what I felt today . . .

Here is what I'm doing to celebrate my results . . .

Day 14

My overall intent for this sacred clutter-clearing journey is . . .

_____

_____

_____

_____

My intent for today's clearing is . . .

_____

_____

_____

_____

My desired physical results for today's journey are . . .

_____

_____

_____

_____

My desired emotional results for today's journey are . . .

_____

_____

_____

_____

Here's what I accomplished today . . .

_____

_____

_____

_____

_____

Here is what I felt today . . .

_____

_____

_____

_____

_____

_____

Here is what I'm doing to celebrate my results . . .

_____

_____

_____

_____

_____

_____

Acknowledgments

Thank you to Kate Hanley for your help in crafting this journal, especially on such a tight schedule. Because of you, it was a smooth process, and we made our deadlines. Thank you to Lara Asher for your editorial direction and development—it has been an immense joy working with you—and to Valerie Brooks for her insightful copyedits.

And to Felicia Messina-D'Haiti and LuAnn Cibik for the their incredible gift of teaching the Linn Method of Clutter Clearing with such grace and kindness. You both open my heart . . . and the hearts of thousands.

About the Author

Denise Linn is an internationally renowned teacher in the field of self-development. She has written 20 books, which are available in 29 languages, including the bestseller *Sacred Space* and the award-winning *Feng Shui for the Soul*. Denise has appeared in numerous documentaries and television shows worldwide and is the founder of the Red Lotus Women's Mystery School, which offers professional certification programs. **www.deniselinn.com**

ALSO BY DENISE LINN

BOOKS

Altars
Dream Lover
*Energy Strands**
*Feng Shui for the Soul**
*Four Acts of Personal Power**
*The Hidden Power of Dreams**
*If I Can Forgive, So Can You**
*Kindling the Native Spirit**
*The Mystic Cookbook (with Meadow Linn)**
*Past Lives, Present Miracles**
*Quest (with Meadow Linn)**
*Sacred Space**
The Secret Language of Signs
*Secrets & Mysteries**
*Soul Coaching***
*The Soul Loves the Truth**
Space Clearing
*Space Clearing A–Z**
*Unlock the Secret Messages of Your Body!**
*21 Days to Explore Your Past Lives**

ORACLE CARDS

*Gateway Oracle Cards**
*Native Spirit Oracle Cards**
*Sacred Destiny Oracle Cards**
*The Sacred Forest Oracle**
*Sacred Traveler Oracle Cards**
Soul Coaching Oracle Cards**

AUDIO PROGRAMS

Angels! Angels! Angels!
Cellular Regeneration
*Complete Relaxation**
Dreams
*Journeys into Past Lives**
Life Force
Past Lives and Beyond
Phoenix Rising
*33 Spirit Journeys**
The Way of the Drum

VIDEO

*Instinctive Feng Shui for Creating Sacred Space**
***

*Available from Hay House
Please visit Hay House UK: www.hayhouse.co.uk; Hay House USA: www.hayhouse.com*;
Hay House Australia: www.hayhouse.com.au; Hay House India: www.hayhouse.co.in

HAY HOUSE TITLES OF RELATED INTEREST

YOU CAN HEAL YOUR LIFE,
the movie, starring Louise Hay & Friends
(available as an online streaming video)
Learn more at www.hayhouse.com/louise-movie

THE SHIFT, the movie,
starring Dr. Wayne W. Dyer
(available as an online streaming video)
Learn more at www.hayhouse.com/the-shift-movie

***

*3 MINUTE POSITIVITY JOURNAL: Boost Your Mood. Train
Your Mind. Change Your Life,* by Kristen Butler

*HOW TO LOVE YOURSELF: A Guided Journal for
Discovering Your Inner Strength and Beauty,* by Louise Hay

*FROM CLUTTER TO CLARITY: Clean Up Your Mindset to
Clear Out Your Clutter,* by Kerri L. Richardson

*CLEAR HOME, CLEAR HEART: Learn to Clear the Energy of
People & Places,* by Jean Haner

*SPIRITUAL ACTIVATOR: 5 Steps to Clearing, Unblocking,
and Protecting Your Energy to Attract More Love, Joy, and
Purpose,* by Oliver Niño

All of the above are available at your local bookstore, or may
be ordered by visiting:

Hay House UK: www.hayhouse.co.uk

Hay House USA: www.hayhouse.com®

Hay House Australia: www.hayhouse.com.au

Hay House India: www.hayhouse.co.in

CONNECT WITH
HAY HOUSE
ONLINE

🌐 hayhouse.co.uk   **f** @hayhouse

📷 @hayhouseuk   𝕏 @hayhouseuk

▶ @hayhouseuk   ♪ @hayhouseuk

Find out all about our latest books & card decks • Be the first to know about exclusive discounts • Interact with our authors in live broadcasts • Celebrate the cycle of the seasons with us • Watch free videos from your favourite authors • Connect with like-minded souls

'*The gateways to wisdom and knowledge are always open.*'

Louise Hay